The Last Wild Place

Other Books by Peter Serchuk

Waiting for Poppa at the Smithtown Diner
All That Remains
The Purpose of Things (with photographer Pieter de Koninck)

The Last Wild Place

Poems by Peter Serchuk

Published by WordTech Editions
P.O. Box 541106
Cincinnati, OH 45254-1106

ISBN: 978-1-62549-473-3

Poetry Editor: Kevin Walzer
Business Editor: Lori Jareo

Visit us on the web at www.wordtechweb.com

For M and J
My heart, My prize.

It's a great life if you don't weaken.

from "Cher Ami and Major Whittlesey"
by Kathleen Rooney

Acknowledgments

American Journal of Poetry: "The Saddest Polar Bear in China,"
"Asylum," "The Morning News in Oslo"
Atlanta Review: "Still Life with Heron and Egret," "The Executioner"
Badlands: "Indian Summer"
Black Fox Literary Magazine: "From the Astronaut's Logbook"
Blast Furnace: "Jeffers, Dying"
Clackamas Literary Review: "Barcelona," "The Man Who Cuts
My Hair"
Cloudbank: "Summer of Love," "Horse"
Concho River Review: "Revising the End"
Connecticut River Review: "At the Tule Elk Reserve,"
"Tourist's Diary"
Crosswinds Poetry Journal: "Chasing My Potential"
Cumberland River Review: "Surfers"
Denver Quarterly: "Full"
Gyroscope Review: "Winter at the Olson Brothers' Orchard"
Innisfree Poetry Journal: "Fire Chasers"
I-70 Review: "Feeding the Birds," "Principles of Welding"
Main Street Rag: "Cowboys in the Modern Age"
Naugatuck River Review: "My Father Knew People," "Minute
by Minute"
New Letters: "Visiting the Master"
New Plains Review: "Conversing with My Shirts"
Passengers Journal: "Car That Can't Resist a Wall"
Paterson Literary Review: "End-of Life Opportunities"
POEM: "On the Lace Lichen Trail, Point Lobos," "Murder
at the Indianapolis Zoo"
Prime Number Magazine: "The Foley Artist"
Tebot Bach Anthology: "Desert Sunrise"
The Cape Rock: "The View from North Dakota," "Inside a
Church Not of Your Own Faith"
The Sow's Ear Poetry Journal: "Lucky"
The Timberline Review: "Lessons in Picking Fruit," "The Last
Wild Place," "Joe's Daughter," "Revelations at the
Desert Fruit Stand"

The Westchester Review: "Dead Bird on the Porch," "Her
    Wicked Curveball"
The Worcester Review: "Not the Man"
Wisconsin Review: "We Were Talking on the Phone
    When My Father Died"

Table of Contents

I.

Cowboys in the Modern Age 17
Conversing with My Shirts 18
The Saddest Polar Bear in China 19
The Man Who Cuts My Hair 20
Inside a Church Not of Your Own Faith 21
The View from North Dakota 22
Barcelona 23
Visiting the Master 24
Full 25
My Father Knew People 26

II.

The Last Wild Place 29
Lessons in Picking Fruit 30
Summer of Love 31
Asylum 32
Minute by Minute 33
Surfers 34
Still Life with Heron and Egret 35
Murder at the Indianapolis Zoo 36
At the Tule Elk Reserve 37
The Morning News in Oslo 38

III.

Chasing My Potential 41
On the Lace Lichen Trail, Point Lobos 42
Desert Sunrise 43

Indian Summer 44

The Foley Artist 45

Her Wicked Curveball 46

Sidelines 47

Dwarf Galaxies 48

Principles of Welding 49

IV.

Dead Bird on the Porch 53

Horse 54

Fire Chasers 55

Tourist's Diary 56

The Executioner 57

Jeffers, Dying 59

Car That Can't Resist a Wall 60

Memory Lake 61

From the Astronaut's Logbook 62

V.

Revelations at the Desert Fruit Stand 65

Lucky 66

Winter at the Olson Brothers' Orchard 67

End-of-Life Opportunities 68

The Cemetery Called Hollywood Forever 69

Feeding the Birds 70

We Were Talking on the Phone When My Father
Died 71

Joe's Daughter 72

Where I Live 73

Not The Man 74
Revising the End 75

I.

Cowboys in the Modern Age

They're mostly vegans now, non-smokers too,
nobody's fool once the cemetery in Marlboro Country
became the biggest home on the range. Those huge
cattle drives too are yesterday's news, no more men
in chaps ushering thundering herds across the plains.
In their place, wranglers now pilot drones from control
rooms miles away, move the Angus and Brahmans
from field to field with the flick of a wrist.
To the herd it's all the same, grunts and gas,
even the smartest oblivious to the pre-recorded
crooning of *Git along, little doggies.*
No matter, after a long day behind a joystick,
cowboys are still ready for a good laugh, a cold beer
and a little George Jones. Then it's off to the gym
for spin class and pilates. Just what every cowpoke
needs to keep his two-step razor sharp out where
the buffalo roam.

Conversing with My Shirts

The shirts in my closet complain
they're too tired for work, yet constantly
this urging toward the next mirage.
In their pockets I find the lint of previous
seasons, old ambitions masquerading
as hunger and thirst. I explain that a mirage
is a fever that conjures the past as the future,
that confuses the blindness of what was with
the blindness of what could be. Unconvinced,
each morning the shirts rattle on their hangers;
mistaking starch for resilience, wrinkles for
wisdom and a light switch for a burning bush.

The Saddest Polar Bear in China

Nine feet long and a thousand pounds
of bone and fleece, he lives in the wilderness
of a Guangzhou mall pacing side-to-side.
Shoppers, faces mesmerized, press against
the glass, as close as they'll come to untamed air.
As if to prove the point, they've named him Pizza.
Pizza, stand! they scream.
Pizza, growl! they shout.
Pizza, over here! Over here! Over here!
But Pizza does not stand or growl as Pizza
is truly sad, for not a single soul watching
has considered the idea that Pizza might be
the Christ reborn, the Krishna reincarnated,
Allah made visible, the Buddha transformed.
Singularly alive in front of arctic murals
and manufactured ice, Pizza surveys
the landscape before his eyes.
Remembering light he breathed to reveal
the earth, fish he blessed to feed the world,
Pizza prays for the billions on the other side:
his blind creation, his dream of perfection,
still lost in the wild.

19

The Man Who Cuts My Hair

The man who cuts my hair has heard it all:
from high and low, the best and worst,
from every perch up and down the ladder.
So each month, for an hour, I hear about the lives
of other men: tales of brokers, actors, lawyers
and accountants. I'd be lying if I said I didn't listen.
Scissors snapping in my ears like castanets, I learn about
the one who struck it rich then bought a curvy, younger wife.
The one who rigged the books and now reads inside a cell.
The one who lived to eat until an artery blew a fuse.
Still, as he cuts and trims, shaves and clips, I can't help
but wonder what tales he tells of me when others take my place.
Some lucky fool with the Midas touch? Or maybe a would-be
hipster too eager to embrace an earring and tattoo.
The list could go on and on, the possibilities endless.
My head now spinning in a dream, I see them all, wearing
my clothes, imposters crowding the mirror. Then I'm back
in the room, eyebrows being trimmed, watching the man
who cuts my hair clean my neck and lower my chair.
You look like a million bucks, he says.
I stand and pay his fee, tip him an extra twenty.
He slaps my back and shakes my hand, as if he knows me.

Inside a Church Not of Your Own Faith

A kind face welcomes you at the door
but the tortured souls on the stained glass
have their doubts. They have a hunch your
savior's in your billfold, that you spend your
nights marking cards, trash-talking the moon.
Still, forgiveness may be in the air,
the way clarity can tap your shoulder when
you least expect it, pointing to a door that
only yesterday looked like a wall.
Don't blow your chance now by asking
for miracles, by asking the man holding
the collection plate if he can make change.
Take what is given with a quiet tongue,
with the humility of a naked branch granted
another season. There may be a thousand
souls you can save just by unclenching
your fist. No one has to know the life you've
lived, the bodies thrown from cliffs, how just
this morning you prayed in front of the mirror,
your eyes wide open.

The View from North Dakota

Southerners have a taste for nostalgia.
It doesn't take more than a balmy breeze
to carry them back to some old house
and a younger face, a distant voice
or a kiss they never washed away.
Southerners don't have families,
they have *their people* and memory is
the shaded porch where their days
are gathered like fresh-cut flowers.

Here in Minot, it's different.
When that first winter blast chases
hands into pockets, when the first snow
grips our boots and reminds us
only angels leave this earth singing,
all we can think about is tomorrow's work
and the heavy walk toward Spring.
It takes all of summer to thaw us out.

And when the leaves of Fall change clothes
once more, some neighbor's bound to say
they've had enough; they cannot bear
another turn. We don't blame them.
We wish them well and say goodbye.
But we do not call and do not write.
In fact, we rarely speak their names
'til years have passed and word arrives
to say they've died.

Barcelona

There is a beautiful place in the mind that rebels;
that one day wakes incensed by the prison of straight lines,
the politics of right angles. Suddenly, everything inside
seems a pantomime of passions while outside, familiar trees
mirror a garden of old ideas. Before you've said a word,
you're suddenly out on your own limb, casting a shadow
unrecognizable even to yourself.

If this happens to be your mind, now may be a perfect time
to visit Barcelona. Built by Romans before Christ descended,
it's been crowded from the beginning and restless ever since.
With your new shadow, you could walk streets that have reinvented
themselves time and again, learn to shout *no més* in perfect Catalan
and fall under the spell of Cases' *Julia* or Fortuny's *Bastián.*
In Barcelona, love and rage sleep in each other's arms.

Then again, the climate is not for everyone. The summer heat
dizzies the eyes and the Mediterranean does little to cool the blood.
Miro's *Pla de l'Os* may put a soul at ease for an afternoon,
but once you're out on a limb, Barcelona is no place for rest.
If the beautiful place in your mind has spoken, if it vows to
never turn back, perhaps it's time to remind yourself, as Gaudí
often did; there's triumph in a certain madness and a vision
remains in every masterpiece, even those left unfinished.

Visiting the Master

I met the master before he died,
his best work behind him,
his eyes colorless and squinting
as if they'd already seen too much.
Nothing changes, he shouted at
whatever mystery was listening.
Then looking back to me, *At least,*
none of the important stuff.
His hands were spotted and his face
a waning shade. Whatever breeze
was in the room was wheezing.
Go ahead and read me something,
so I did. He listened and he snored,
then insisted that I read a couple more.
Afterward we shuffled through the garden
and the fruit trees. We listened to magpies
as the sun burnt down. He mentioned
wise, sweet Horace, as if he'd seen him
yesterday. He cleared his throat of smoke
and sang a little Roethke. On the porch
his wife brought cookies and Glenlivet.
I fumbled with my notebook and thanked
him one more time. *You won't strike gold*
chasing down old men like me, he said.
There's hope for you but keep it short.
God's patience isn't what it used to be.

Full

They said he'd had a full life
as if it had reached its brim;
the wine savored, thirst quenched
and now he was ready to sleep.
And I suppose they could be right
as people tire of so many things
once cherished: places, friends,
the one-time love of their life.
Still, I've sat with the dying, some
brittle with age, others too young
to be riddled with disease and felt
them squeeze my hand grateful to
know someone was still there.
Or maybe to plead that the glass
was not yet full enough and maybe,
just maybe, that I could somehow
pull them back.

My Father Knew People

My father knew people.
In a handshake he could separate
the thieves from the saints; some high
on the rung, some down in the street.
And he put none above the other so
the well of his friends ran wide and deep.
And friends do things for friends others
won't do. So, when Tony came to see him,
afraid for his life, they talked in whispers
almost airtight. Listening hard by the stairs,
I heard enough to understand: a man with
a gun in Tony's yard, night after night,
threatening to kill Tony, his kids and wife.
I'd never heard a grown man cry before—
an underwater sound, bubbles instead of breath.
My father listened, left to make a call
and when he came back I tried to hear more
but my eyes were lead. Fifteen years passed
before I told my father what I'd heard.
Tony had died from a stroke the previous year.
About the man with the gun?
My father shook his head. *A terrible thing*
to threaten a man's wife and kids.
I waited to hear more as I had on the stairs.
My father shook his head again.
Let's just say he disappeared.

II.

The Last Wild Place

I keep searching for it,
not in the world but in myself,
that abandoned universe
where the sun has not yet shackled
itself to depreciating currency,
where the moon still saves
a thread of light for whatever
wager seems hopeless.

I live in the world and drink
its wine, a man praised
and scorned for all his disguises.
But there are nights like this
when the wind lays down its head,
when somewhere far off, I hear
nostrils trumpet and feel under
my skin the fever of the Appaloosa,
Paint and Morgan as they trample
the gate and fly into the night
on the heels of Przewalski's horse.

Lessons in Picking Fruit

1.
With peaches, women do it best.
Or a man who's learned from gentleness
a sweeter thing may come. You start
with open palm, as if gravity's smallest
soul had lighted on the hand. Only then
do fingers close, barely resting on
the globe, then a gentle tug as if bringing
your only child into the world.

2.
For pears, bring strong legs,
a stubborn back, and a ladder sure as
any friend. Each load is 30 pounds,
basket after basket, up and down
all day. The sap's like glue, every insect
loves your eyes and despises something
human size thieving in their world.
After a day of pears, you'll have earned
your rest; your meal, your bath
and a few cold beers.

3
Now cherries are like poodles,
high strung and full of need. But once
they've swelled into their sweetness,
fingers learn the hard way they don't
wish to leave their tree. The stems
are like barbed wire when you pull
the clusters clean; wounds every man
forgets once the sweet pit curls his tongue.

Summer of Love

If you come to San Francisco
Summertime will be a love-in there.

It's hard to imagine now, in the shadows
Of this world, something called The Summer of Love.
Yet, had you been there, a ghost on a lamp post
Or a small cloud overhead, you might have seen
And heard and felt for yourself what was in the air.
True, you might have taken in more than a few breaths
Of Acapulco Gold and passed a few freaks visiting
A distant planet on LSD. Naturally, that's what made
The news, what America saw, the networks parroting
Each other with Hippie this and Flower People that,
Seeing everything, as always, through yesterday's eyes.
But had you been there, your own eyes clear, you might
have said it was more about the future than the freaks,
If nothing more than a dream of the future, imagining
A world built on something other than ways and means.
The dreamers were young and naïve, their eyes too fixed
To see peripherally. And it was just a summer, one short
Season; not so different from the short seasons of others
Who've dreamed and knew the price of such dreaming.
So what followed was bitter learning: the assassinations of '68,
The Kent State killings in '70, Nixon, Watergate and all the rest.
The future reverting to the mean. And so we live in *this* world,
In the shadows of our own creation and wait for the new
Dreamers, for another summer to awaken in all of us.

Asylum

Asylum for the Relief of Persons Deprived of the Use of Their Reason
Opened May 15, 1817

Leave it to the good souls of Quakers to see through
the early fog of days ahead. Hanged, beaten and chased
from Massachusetts by Puritans, they parachuted into
Rhode Island and Pennsylvania already wise about the ways
a stew of politics and faith can short-circuit a brain.
But that was only one of many dangerous recipes
already on the stove. The infant country, head swollen
from independence and suddenly aware of its arms
and legs, had jumped into no less than eight wars since
the British sailed home. And wars with the Seminoles,
Cherokee and Sauks were straight ahead. It was enough
to deprive civilized men of their reason, to find themselves
surrounded by so many *patriots* who'd forgotten the what
and why of the ground they stood on, decided all land
was theirs for taking, white the master of the rainbow.
A heady time indeed. Appetites ran amok. Barely a thought
to step back and ask, *What God taught this to us?*
Surely not the one others called insane and hammered
to a cross. So blessed be the Quakers for these doors
swung open wide. What better time to step inside with
those who dream out loud; who converse with empty walls
and sometimes, without harm, only soil themselves.

Minute by Minute

In 1953, "H.M." underwent an experimental brain operation in Hartford to correct a seizure disorder, only to emerge from it fundamentally and irreparably changed. He had lost the ability to form new memories. For the next 55 years, each time he met a friend, each time he ate a meal, each time he walked in the woods, it was as if for the first time.
The Case of "H.M." McGill University

If you say you are my friend, I'll believe you,
if only for a minute. Those who've been betrayed
by a handshake or kiss can only wish they'd been
so lucky. I can be told neither truth nor lie.
All history melts into the air. I have no lost loves,
no riches squandered, no dreams blackened by regret.
Time cannot mock me.
I'm news to myself every day.
In truth, it's you I pity, for all that you must carry;
years of grief, clouds of doubt and disappointment,
the numbness of boredom and routine. For me nothing
is habit, soiled or missed. I wake each morning God's
new man on Earth, witness to the first sunrise, the music
of each voice and note thrilling my ear. I'm here in each
moment newly minted, a diary of blank pages, all doubts
and fears vanished by day's end. Still, make no mistake,
we see the same stars and sky. And if you call me brother,
if you say you love me, I'll treasure it always.
Even if always is only for a minute.

Surfers

At the funeral for his surfer son who'd fallen
from a wall, I joined the line of mourners who
shuffled forward with nothing wise to say.
His eyes were dry, a lifetime of tears exiled
for another day. On the beach below, the surf
was up, rolling hills of green and blue.
A single board stood upright in salute while
his son's friends paddled out and glided in,
their wetsuits like sealskin liquid in the sun.
When my turn came to share his grief, we each
reached for the other's shoulders, locked eye to eye.
"You don't have to be so tough," I whispered behind
his mask. He nodded as if I'd complimented his tie.
"It's a beautiful day to be on a board," he answered,
as if still grateful to be alive.

Still Life with Heron and Egret

If the horses from my hand didn't impersonate cows
and my cows not so easily mistaken for rectangles with feet,
I'd probably be here at Whaler's Cove with a sketchbook
giving this blue heron and snowy egret the artistic merit
they deserve. Not that they care either way;
the heron's perched on a piece of driftwood, staring off
into the future, the egret not ten feet away balanced
on a bathmat of sea kelp. As they bob ever-so-slightly
on the slow breathing of the tide, I'm guessing art means
less to them than a place where they can rest undisturbed,
unconcerned about their place in the universe or whether
they might be remembered fondly for the small footprint
they'll leave on a darkening wave. Or perhaps they know
more about art than one might guess. Though they barely
move, I'm now convinced their stance is more like poetry
than painting; recalling a famous poet's wisdom that a poem
should not mean, but be.

Murder at the Indianapolis Zoo

His first thought might have been *heat*
but the season was wrong despite the wildness
in her eyes. Still, she paced, closer each time,
the cubs out of sight, her twitching tail an electric
surprise, enough to rouse any king from half-sleep.
Then again, how simple the mind of men and kings.
In less than a blink she has him pinned on his back,
paws on his throat, teeth at his neck. He tries rolling
her off, clubbing her head but her paws press too hard,
her teeth dig deeper, the competing roars ignite a hellish
choir of shrieks and screams, zookeepers racing from
every corner but helpless to short-circuit what instinct
has commanded. Within minutes, all is quiet,
order restored; the king is dead. Not bled to death
but choked to death, the work of a master killer.
Yet, what to make of this? In eight years, not a scratch
nor squabble, their lives together comfortable and well fed,
no muddy stream of human dreams or regrets.
And look now, the cubs creeping back to their
mother's side; a passing glance at their father's
empty shell, no longer strangers to the wild.

At the Tule Elk Reserve

No fools for bad weather, Tule Elk live only
in California where the seasons keep them free
of a winter wardrobe and the political climate
spares them the hallucinations of poachers.
In return, they patrol their grasslands, mindful
to keep non-native shrubs on the run.

Coming up the western side of the Tamales Reserve,
where the trail looks down on the welcome mat
of the great Pacific, I see them on the ridge above;
the bull with his royal crown silhouetted against the sun
and nearby, the harem under his protection.

It's not long before he sees me too, an unwelcome intruder.
To get a better look, he moves forward to size me up;
a scrawny creature on two legs, not a quarter of his weight,
no match for a duel with his antler swords. He offers me
the choice: come forward like the other bulls he has broken
or turn back and leave him to his peace.

Of course how is he to know there is nothing to fear from me?
Armed only with curiosity, here I am the one unprotected,
the species more likely to be the hunted than the hunter.
And yet, the Tule do not hunt, they only protect,
model citizens of the world.

Slowly, I step back, step by step, let the bull know I am
not here to challenge but merely to observe, to lift my ears
to the reveille of his bugling; which is not a call to arms
but a reminder to the harem that August and September
are fine months for mating.

The Morning News in Oslo

I read the morning news as if I'm in Oslo,
sipping akevitt at the Grand Café, a river
of sunlight coursing down Karl Johans Gate
while Norse gods sway in their blue hammock
above the shimmering fjord.

How sad, I think, for my brethren back home;
the war between the states still raging,
vigilantes of lost dreams now guarding
the palaces they'll only get to clean,
generations of grudges still crouched over
an imaginary ball.

New friends stop by to say hello, armed with
cloudberries, krumkake, lupines and heather.
They glance at headlines over my shoulder
and ask politely, in broken English,
What flowers still grow in America?

III.

Chasing My Potential

Like a racehorse, I've spent a lifetime exhausting myself,
trying to shorten the distance between us. As often as
I've sprinted, ears back, eyes wide with determination,
other times I've let myself jog, walk or even sit, wiping
potential's dust from my face. There have been days
when I thought I could catch him, when the right word,
the right dream, all seemed within reach. Yet despite
the sweat, the pep talks with God, sooner or later I'd
watch him disappear into the impossible. And now,
the chase long over, I carry his memory on my back
like a dead soldier, not so much as an admission of failure
but as a reminder that the sooner I bury him,
the happier I'll be.

On the Lace Lichen Trail, Point Lobos

If you need to weep for the dead
or the deaf ear of the world, here
you'll find a timeless shoulder waiting.
Monterey pines and coast live oak stand
draped in the silk of green-grey lichen
as if bearded with old wisdom or streaming
sympathetic tears. Then again, if joy is
the life jacket for all dark seas, rejoice
in the wild iris and red amanita that grow
underneath, the arias harbor seals sing
so close to shore and the knowledge that
the Costanoans used this ancient fleece
to dress their wounds and diaper their young.

Desert Sunrise

Behind me, California sleeps,
the toast barely up in Albuquerque,
the coffee lukewarm in Omaha,
Detroit already revealed for
everything it will never be.
But here, snakes and scorpions
glory in the waking of uncivilized
streets, saguaros stand against
all logic and history repeats
its riddle of raucous silence.
A black widow combs her web,
the elf owl sleeps with one eye open,
Harris hawks and diamondbacks
play chess with careless mice—
none of them guessing at love,
none measuring forgiveness,
not one single creature raging
at heaven for a life incomplete
or a home by the sea.

Indian Summer

Seasons know their time
and yet like a desperate heart
already underwater, this one
reaches back to grab hold
of the sinking line.
Still, losses must be tallied
however silent the grieving,
September's wild leaves
scattered to the ground.
And this face too, a stranger
in the mirror, reaches back to
rescue what was felt and known;
light that was seen in all its
green disguises. So, praise be
the days ahead, that they don't
arrive too soon. And praise be
the blindfold of Indian Summers,
endless nights of stars and moons.

The Foley Artist

By now you know the charge of the stallion
is just me slapping wooden blocks.
The growling thunder, bowling balls on a cement floor
and those wet kisses that can't bear to say goodbye—
suction cups my fingers walk across a vaselined mirror.
It's all for good, isn't it? Alone in the dark, so much
of what we need to hear would otherwise disappear
as our eyes race ahead. And then there are the sounds
unheard. That demands a special craft: the laughter of
misplaced friends, cracked horns of ships that won't come
in, the dirge of a lock to a different life rusted on its chain.
So what if it's just me on a soundstage with whistles
and brooms? Me with chopsticks, bubble wrap and spoons
shooting sparks into the memory of forgotten years?
Driving home, you'll replay the only soundtrack worth
remembering, all those things left behind in silence;
the whisper of the heart's lost planets, guardian angels
repeating your name—all this and more, once more,
alive in your ears.

Her Wicked Curveball

Some said it was the break, impossible to read,
as if a sudden breeze grabbed it by the neck
spinning it east or west before shoving it
south into gravity's mouth. Impossible to read,
they said. More than impossible to hit.

Still, I dug myself in, armed with years of
practice swings and enough broken bats
to make me wise about such things. I locked
my eyes on her eyes searching for a clue,
ready for that pitch others had swung through.

Ah, but love is not a game, not for those
who lose. The heart in heat always flies to
the farthest fence. Never mind the sun
in your eyes, the thinning crowd, afternoon
shadows creeping across the mound.

She took her signs from one I could not see,
one who knew the score oblivious to me.
Then kicked her leg and cocked her arm
all with a loving sigh. Then disappeared without
a trace as I watched her final pitch sail by.

Sidelines

Easy to sit like a statue while the world spins out of control
but not for Tommy Lewis. From where he sits on the sidelines,
adrenaline pumping his blood into overdrive, the world seems
perched on a ledge. After all, this is the Alabama Crimson Tide
and he is their co-captain. The same Crimson Tide that crushed
Syracuse in the Orange Bowl just last year. Yet here they are in
the '54 Cotton Bowl already trailing Rice. And now it's Rice's ball
on their own five when their All-American halfback Dicky Maegle
takes the handoff and flies up the Alabama sideline like a runaway
train. Nothing's going to catch him: not a linebacker or safety,
not Mercury himself. But this injustice cannot stand. Not for
Tommy Lewis. His patience melted down, he bolts like a madman
from the bench, flies onto the field and before you've blinked, takes
Dicky Maegle down at the Alabama 42. The crowd's in a frenzy,
benches screaming, the order of the universe in disarray.
Dicky Maegle's dazed but Tommy's mind is clear.
"What's the worst that can happen, a penalty for interference?"
But the referee sees the spinning world from a different perch.
When the center falls apart, someone must stitch it back in place.
Incensed, he throws the yellow flag and makes his call; he grants
Maegle and Rice another touchdown. Some cheer, some boo,
some call Tommy a fool but he has no regrets. The Tide's odyssey
at stake, he took a chance and did what had to be done. The favor
of the gods might have saved the day as it sometimes does. But on
this day the gods demurred. They chose Dicky Maegle as their
Ulysses and the Owls from Rice easily won.

Dwarf Galaxies

When the soul is under siege, when the world
discounts your measure in the world, it's helpful
to remind yourself of the dwarf galaxies, originally
discarded as celestial dust and gas. Take Draco,
for example, a small hammock in the side yard of
the Milky Way, hundreds of light years wide, cradling
billions of stars. Still, Albert George Wilson thought
the word "dwarf" best captured the size and significance
of Draco and its siblings—while Wilson, conversely,
was thought to be a "giant" among his fellow astronomers.
And yet today there is not the smallest particle trace of
Albert George Wilson anywhere in the universe while Draco
and its fellow dwarfs continue to expand like a belly laugh
and their basket of stars shine on and on and on.

Principles of Welding

Mr. Gunderson taught philosophy
disguised as metal shop. His favorite topic:
principles of welding. *Temperatures*
must be hot, he'd begin, *hotter than*
all resistance, the heat inversely
proportional to cold, hard facts.
We'd show him key chains, lockets
and boxes for who knows what.
With metals, he'd say, *it's a matter*
of science, insisting molecules coalesce.
Then, there's the human mind, too easily
bound to calculation and grandeur,
as if what begs for welds must instead
be hammered. Shop was required,
but we took it for laughs, three hours
a week with torches, glasses and piles
of metal scrap. No grades, just pass
or fail and Gunderson's sly wit.
A perfect weld demands a heart,
he'd say. *Boys, keep the fire hot.*
Civilization depends on it.

IV.

Dead Bird on the Porch

Too lost in song or the joy of his wings,
perhaps he did not see the glass door.
Or perhaps he did, and seeing his reflection,
was unhappy with what he saw; not the hawk
or condor he imagined, his small life more
than he could bear. The world weighs heavy
on those with open eyes, who travel far,
see so much, then look inside.

I gathered him up in the morning news
like a stillborn infant placed at my door,
careful to not disturb what had already
been wrecked. Laying him gently in a hole
of dirt and twigs, wrapped in headlines of
politics and wars, one could only guess what
waits ahead of our own quick wings;
a path above trees or our own glass door.

Horse

How fast my horse can run, I cannot say.
I've never given him free rein or if I have
there's a point beyond which he will not go,
will not test the limits of his imagination.

He's a proud horse, well bred, with a thick
mane and a sleek build. In any light his coat
shimmers like a river of dark pearls. He's been
loved from the moment his hooves hit ground.

Still, I wonder if it's love or the imagination
that has its limits. Together in the barn, I can
only guess which of us is sleeping standing up,
which heart truly dreams of a field without a fence.

Fire Chasers

In the next canyon the fires are fierce.
Winds hurl their lasso hill to hill, gorging on brush,
hissing like snakes, a streak of tigers leaping walls
and ravines to hunt down the houses below.
Road signs warn us to keep out but we can't contain
our own heat. So we drive in through the closed park,
up the tire-chewing backroad until we kill the engine
and roll to a stop just blocks from the flashing lights.
We inch our way closer. What is it we've come to see?
Firehawks water-bomb slopes, police cars barricade streets
while armies of yellow and red attack with their axes,
ladders and hoses block by block, house by house.
The sky is surreal, Van Gogh's *Starry Night* turned
orange and black. We fight back the smoke and heat,
live in the sweat, throats raw, eyes bloodshot. We hide
in the pandemonium. Minutes pass. Two hours pass.
Soon the wind begins to doze and more trucks unwind
their hoses to seize the upper hand. The curtain of smoke
sways then lifts, reveals the ghost of a neighborhood.
No longer invisible, firefighters see us and our teary eyes,
take us for homeowners suddenly homeless, possessions
reduced to memory and ash. Some nod their sympathy,
offer their regrets. We can't bear to speak the truth,
ashamed to be spellbound by the misery of others.
We lower our heads, wait until the street begins to clear
then slip back into the dark, into our car, back to our safe
and quiet home, repeating over and over, each to the other,
Everything's going to be alright.

Tourist's Diary

Everyone knows I'm just passing through.
My clothes don't match the weather and
my voice is out of tune with the local pitch.
Yet kindness is easy to come by when
small talk is the common currency.
Still, I make a mistake when I'm asked,
"What brings you here?" and answer,
"Curiosity." By that I mean a hunger for
something born from a different palette,
not a history that won't sleep or ghosts
that still patrol the streets. Some say
the future is often the past with different faces.
I'm not sure though back where I'm from
we have ghosts of our own and stains that
have never come clean. Little wonder tourists
there are greeted with a similar kindness
and the same practiced smile; delighted to see
them come and grateful to watch them go.

The Executioner

"After man survives hanging, Iran plans a second attempt"
        News Item

The eyes are full of illusions, this we know,
nearsighted to dragons in the distance,
farsighted to angels at our elbow.
No, the eyes cannot be trusted, yet
I watched this man die for that is how
I feed my children. As you drive your bus,
hammer your nails, as you shuffle the clouds
of each day's routine so I peer through my hood,
place another over each man's head, bring
the knot of the noose to the side of his neck
and whisper: *Go now to a better world.*
And so it is and so it was, the lever pulled,
the floor disappearing under feet, the body,
a lifetime, dropping until the rope said *Stop!*
Unmasking myself, I took him down,
man to man. I took what the soul discards
and carried it to the room to be cleansed
and made holy for the earth.
What happened next is still a dream.
I laid him down, removed the hood,
but as I turned away a sound slid through
his throat like the hissing of a snake.
The curtains of his eyes inched open,
pupils pulsing on pools of blood.
I screamed, stood back. His lungs clawed
for air. He gasped and coughed and spit.
Brother, he choked, *am I alive or dead?*
Stunned, I did not answer presently,
for in that moment I feared that if he were
the man alive then I must be the dead.
Brother, he asked, *are you an angel?*
I sat him up and brought him water
though I knew he could not swallow.
I placed wet cloths on the raw peel
of his neck. He stared deep into my eyes
like a child newly born into the world.

And I wept as if he were my child,
wept at the grace of God, wept
knowing the state and knowing his fate.
We've met before, he said as I held
him in my arms. *Yes,* I answered.
Yes, brother, in another lifetime.

Jeffers, Dying

Tor House, 1962

From my bed by the window
I hear the ocean stand and fall.
The light's too dim now, day or night,
so my ears and nose must guess the hour
and gather wood for dreaming.
And yet no dreamer built this home,
this quarry ship and Gaelic tower.
Each stone in place knew this shoulder
and this shoulder every weight. You don't
build a home of rock from gentleness.
Everything I am was built from love and rage.
I screamed in stone to keep the nightmares at bay.
This ocean was my heart, my trapped
and brooding twin. I won't miss this world,
and its manic ways, just the memory of
one woman in her tower. And this ocean,
fouled for the sake of man, pounding its fist
on the door of the day.

Car That Can't Resist a Wall

We're driving as fast as we can
on the road called Great Tomorrow.

Road signs rise up like ghosts to shout
warnings, but we ignore them.

Bullets fly past the windshield
whistling *God Bless America*.

There are fires in the rear-view mirror
but that's so yesterday's news.

It's been raining for days, but why worry?
The Good Lord promised no more floods.

People by the roadside flag us down
but we know how to blur their faces.

The radio screams, *Stop! Go back!*
so we turn the dial to Elvis.

We're driving as fast as we can
on the road called Great Tomorrow.

When we close our eyes we can see
a future nobody will forget.

Memory Lake

We think of going back.
We remember how the wind would circle
the shore, the sun climbing its ladder
reminding us to hold our tongues until
what seemed clear was truly clear.
Like others, we'd become blind to things
we once scorned, astonished how easily
the world welded us to dreams we thought
were our own. We wonder now if there is
still time to dream old dreams again.
The lake is still there. In our ears we hear
the wail of the loons, see cattails swaying
to the chant of the breeze. Yes, the lake
is still there waiting, waiting. Maybe.

From the Astronaut's Logbook

As seen from space, Earth appears
a quiet place, a modest mass
minding its business, lovely
with its scarf of blue and white.
Here, in the silent swirl of stars,
where the sun is a soothing nightlight
proclaiming all is safe and well,
we take a deep breath, forget
the garden and the viper,
imagine we are none the wiser.

V.

Revelations at the Desert Fruit Stand

Every desert has dreams,
so reads the makeshift sign swaying in the afternoon breeze,
hanging by a lone nail near the front door. Once inside, I begin
to wonder what those dreams could be. The boy behind the counter
shrugs his shoulders like a puppet, says he's never even noticed.
"You should go and ask my mother."
He points to a woman near the bins of pomegranates.
No stranger to the desert, her skin is native bronze.
It seems the sign was left with all the crates years ago
when she bought the place—too curious to throw away.
She sees my disappointment.
"You were probably wishing for some Hopi lore
but it's nothing I've ever heard before."
So, she weighs my trove of apricots and figs. I thank her
for her fruit and time. As she hands me change, she offers this:
"You might ask the chiefs who know the desert best."
Lighting up, I ask who that might be. With a devilish smile
she answers, "Why, Abraham, Moses, and Jesus."

Lucky

You have to be lucky
to have the night at your feet,
the wind in its cave and nearby,
an old cat dreaming of sardines.
You have to be lucky to be so quiet,
to empty your ear of the gossip
and chatter, to hear a river hum
in the distance.

There is so much to be done
before another day can be welcomed;
so many welds to be tested and wounds
to be dressed. You have to be lucky
to know which piece of the moon
still shines on you, which angels
haven't jumped ship yet.

Winter at the Olson Brothers' Orchard

The peach and cherry trees are fast asleep,
the muscled arms of the pear trees heavy with snow.
And down below, the sawmill silent, the lone witness
to the whispers of the Columbia River.

Inside, we sit around the fireplace drinking cider
and talk about the sweat-filled days of August;
hours spent high in the trees, mosquitos jabbing at
our faces, fingers raw from stems not eager to let go.

It was a good season, we say. The orchard broke even
and then some, with enough left over to fix the sprayer.
Sure, we'd hoped for more, but still a hell of a year,
remembering our sore backs and baskets full of jewels.

Now it's time for us to let go, to empty our glasses
and think about winter work down in Spokane or
across the Cascades. We've got months to dream
before Spring, to let the snow fall where it may.

End-of-Life Opportunities

"Prayers for my friend who is dying and embracing end-of-life opportunities"
                    Pastor comments at a Sunday service

Remember the early light on the porch
should you wake in a dark tunnel.

Imagine yourself a blanket of fog
nursing the souls of a thousand trees.

Bless the dog that never judged you
and the cat that spoke in riddles.

Memorize the faces you love should you
arrive strangers in another lifetime.

With your children gathered around you
tell each a secret they can keep forever.

Let all who visit touch your face so
they may carry it always in their hands.

Prepare yourself to be unmasked
as the jailer of your own regrets.

Praise whichever God calls you forward
and strips you of your shame.

The Cemetery Called Hollywood Forever

"Resting Place of Hollywood's Immortals"

We spend our Sunday with the stars however faint
their light might be. The red carpet's gone, along
with the paparazzi, but that doesn't stop us from
racing after Tyrone Power, Fay Wray and Valentino.
Forever's a democracy so the voice of Bugs Bunny
is just a stroll away from Cecil B. Demille, while the
stone-cold likeness of Johnny Ramone jams eternally
across from Mr. Fairbanks Sr and his skirt-chasing son.
Nothing in Los Angeles is ancient ground.
In 1899, after John Truman Gower reaped the last
of his wheat, they turned the soil and began planting
the dead. Chaplin's mother was among the first.
Then a glittering sky of constellations big and small—
Victor Fleming, Norma Talmadge, Marion Davies and
those little rascals, Darla Hood and Carl "Alfalfa" Switzer.
Janet Gaynor, Judy Garland and Peter Lorre all took
their final bows here, knowing Hollywood's not such
a bad place to spend forever. A real field of dreams
between RKO and Paramount, crews joked that when
you died in pictures, when your career was ashes,
they simply threw you over the fence.

Feeding the Birds

My hands are pale but able.
When I offer to put them to work for the food bank,
they politely ask I write them checks instead.
Likewise, the good souls at the homeless shelter
prefer I carry my weight in dollars and leave it
to them to carry the rest. Discouraged, I oblige
nevertheless, grateful that my checkbook has grace
to spare. Still, these hands seem wasted tending only
to the needs of obligation and routine.
And so, I feed the birds.
Twice a day spread seeds across the railing high above
the dreams of mice and squirrels. And on cue, they come:
sparrows, finches, juncos and jays—troubadours, wanderers
and hip-hop artists, lighting from oak trees on the hill below,
mindful of the keen eyes of hawks and the bluster of crows.
Still, I'm nothing to them, just another shadow instinct warns
them to be wary of. Our bargain is simple; I lay down the seeds,
disappear from sight, and they bring me their beauty—
never seeing my face or asking the price of my affection.
For others I've loved, beautiful too, I've sometimes set that
price too high. But for the birds, my hands are at their service.
I feed them and they owe me nothing.

We Were Talking on the Phone When
My Father Died

We were talking on the phone when my father died.
Halfway across the country, in the town I couldn't wait
to leave, he was explaining why he preferred Mahler to Bach,
the deafness of the right and left, and why the salary cap
in football is nothing more than wage control to keep
rich owners rich. While his mind was like a clock that refused
to miss a beat, his body took note of the time, its clock unwinding
pill after pill, year after year. Still, he was here, ranting about
the criminals in Washington, upstate weather and the cloud of days
without my mother or beer. Then he asked how I was feeling, asked
about work and reminded me how lucky I was to live the life I live.
You've been lucky too, I said, surprised when he didn't make a sound.
And lucky me got to say I love you before his phone fell to the ground.

Joe's Daughter

Joe wants me to marry his daughter
but he doesn't know the kind of man I am.
She is sweet like the cherry wine Norwegians
sip at Christmas and I am the bitter grinds of
yesterday's coffee. She tells me she loves me,
again and again, parading the terror of her
gentleness through my imagination. I fear
it's the bitterness she loves but each time
I warn her she takes off her clothes.
Her skin smells like hay after summer rain,
waking every creature in the field.

Joe wants me to marry his daughter
but he doesn't know the kind of man I am.
I come from a good family, so he assumes I am good.
I read books by wise men, so he assumes I am wise.
I say kind things in his house, so he assumes I am kind.
But the rain is good, freed from the hurricane.
And the saint is wise, miles from temptation.
And the witch is kind while she heats the oven.
When I tell this to his daughter, she bites my ear
and sings like the finch in our tree.

Joe wants me to marry his daughter
but he doesn't know the kind of man I am.
His faith's too whole for this cracked-egg world,
proclaiming each day more right than not.
He likes to dance across a room like Fred Astaire.
When I speak of all the armies I've deserted, he fills
my glass and calls me a patriot. A man can only take
so much praise. Little wonder I begin to ponder
if he's right. Have I underestimated the elasticity
of the soul? Can a man morph into another man
better than the man he knows? Maybe just the man
to marry his precious daughter, that silky caterpillar
with a hundred loving arms. I'd have to watch my step,
love's such a slippery ledge and she's wild and free
as any shooting star. Yet sweet like the cherry wine
Norwegians drink at Christmas. And mad enough
to taste something sweet in bitter grinds.

Where I Live

Wild turkeys gather under oak trees in
early morning, deer take their place
in late afternoon. And in the night, under
crescent moons, owls guard the gates of
our sacred kingdom. People say, "You live
in Paradise." Still, nothing much happens here.
Grasses sometime sway, light rains caress
the fields and snow stays high in the mountains—
a reminder of winters elsewhere. Down below,
fish follow the will of the river and days repeat
themselves like waves that kneel at the shore.
Yet ours is a restless contentment, blessed beyond
doubt, but impatient always to hear the voice of
the God that brought us here.

Not The Man

I'm not the man who hears
a train waking in the distance,
who knows by its pitch the familiar
stops it will soon ignore.

I'm not the man who oils
the tracks or readies the switch,
who lights the crowd then calms
their fears, stamping tickets.

By the time I arrive nearly
everyone's guessed the destination,
bid up the real estate and raced
out of yesterday's shoes.

By the time I arrive it seems
years have passed, the station empty.
On the tracks the hum of memories
and yesterday's news.

I'm the man in the plaid shirt
and loose pants, the one painting
a picture of a drive-thru town, of
a lightning train once glory bound.

I'm the man in the plaid shirt
and loose pants, the one angels
tease from time to time,
sweeping up what's left behind.

Revising the End

All things point to the end,
men with hammers in search of nails.
Clear to see pole stars slipping farther
away, to know songbirds warm the heart
while vultures own the cliffs.
And yet what is left of the heart once
it carves out its own shell? Clutching
the gravestones of things vanished denies
the living soul its domain, the human divine.
Yes, horses are rearing their heads
on the carousel, the swallowed tongues
of conscience deafening the moral ear.
And while the die may be cast, it's still
not dry. So let us sing for the soul that claws
its way toward a light it cannot see. And sing
for the heart that can push the darkness deep
into its pockets without breaking stride—
knowing all things point to the end
but insisting it not be the end.

Peter Serchuk's poems have appeared in a variety of journals including *Poetry, American Poetry Review, Hudson Review, Paris Review, North American Review, Boulevard, South Carolina Review, New Plains Review, Atlanta Review, Valparaiso Poetry Review* and many others. In addition, a number of his poems have been anthologized. His published collections are *Waiting for Poppa at the Smithtown Diner* (University of Illinois Press), *All That Remains* (WordTech Editions), and *The Purpose of Things* (Regal House Publishing). More at peterserchuk.com.

.

Made in the USA
Middletown, DE
27 July 2025

10621096R00050